it gets cold

Published by Trident Press
940 Pearl St., Boulder, CO 80302

Front cover art by Mallory Whitten.

ISBN: 978-0-9992499-2-5

it gets cold

j.avery

山

Trident Press
Boulder, CO

*"...as I was saying and I say it again/ so much life and never! And so many years,/ and always much always, always, always!"*
-César Vallejo

*poetics for an open body—*


a corpse without corpus


a corpus without boundaries
        *(end all borders now!)*


a body as a space
both inhabited and inhabiting


the ghost of a ghost


the house and the haunting of the house

the body as a line of
flight
away from the body


*how to be a ghost*—



in search of empty space
learning a type of *dis*-inhabitation

vacated anywhere
you go and there you are –

the ghost is not the being
who dismantles herself


the ghost is the being
who is mantled with herself


*what is a ghost—*
some things move
around on their own
some things move
their own around
it could be that all
movements are

the result of ghosts

the house and the haunting
whose house
certainly not mine
not all ghosts are
anticapitalists but it
helps


anywhere you go
and there you are

space as broken
up by fractured
bodies –

proximity as necessity
but burdened with it
great care and great
motion slip the shape
of this room into
brokenness or
exuberance

oh frictionless spirit
body of its own fracture and
escape
slip into the light some


*rule number one of being a ghost—*

there is no difference at all
between the suggestion of a window
and a window itself


the window is a site(sight)
that masks itself with itself

we cannot see a window
we can only see with a window

the window as a stained-glass:

what is on the outside
of a stained glass window:

the
same thing as the inside
        *light*

we can imagine the space
between
not as a thoroughfare
to the space-not-between
but as an occupational zone

the ghost

is the one who
sees herself
in a stained glass mirror

*rule number two of being a ghost—*

move as though space
do not move as through space

disinhabitation
is the space
where all spatialized metaphors
break down
this body-not-body

we carry each of us

a spatial metaphor
forgive me this


an empty space – for filling


a wound – for healing


a coldness or
a warmth
to feel the coldness or the warmth
find comfort in a temperature
and the sharing of a temperature


a body as a house
for haunting

a body may
inhabit its space of inhabitation


a ghost inhabits
a space of disinhabitation


a restlessness


can an empty space be filled
with another sort of
empty space


*rule number three of being a ghost—*
practical suggestions for haunting

the space you fill



suggests



the space you do not
or cannot
fill

two empty clamshells
on each bank of this river

"                                              "

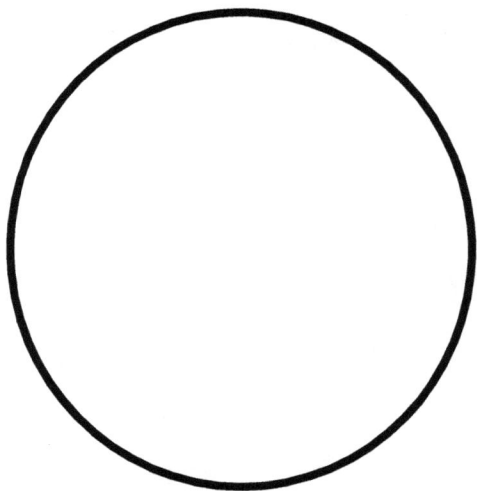

you
must

touch
space

in some
capacity

but

which                              space

*rule number four of being a ghost—*

this
body of ours

is
placed

at the
margins

the
body that
touches space

but can
see the space
where space does
not touch space over
there where the line ends
                    how can these bodies make
                        sense of the spaceless
                            space it learns to
                                in due time
                                    occupy


                    ?

*rule number five of being a ghost—*


queer
descended the same root
as "thwart"

queerness that is athwart
a thwarted queer
(thwart *adj.* situated or placed across some-
thing else)

queerness is
necessarily situated
across or between
something-else

(life/death or
place/void why
not?
)

ghostliness is situated
here too

a sense of something-else
being between
or tangential to the body

a sense of death
as a space
i am situated across
or between

not as a bridge no
or a rope in the
breeze

similar to the throw
how i could be thrown
the act of throwing
across a void
i am thrown
across a void
like a shout or
something like
a horizon
or heavy air

the space between
two tangents
/ /

*rule number six of being a ghost—*

there is a great danger in portraying the queer
as the ghost, the queer body as a body athwart
to death.

there is great potential too.

it is a natural move to place the queer ghost
as a bridge between life and death, space and
not-space, at this point in our exploration of
ghostliness.

we risk re-embodying social structures that, also naturally or under the guise of nature, place the queer body as the closest to death, the non-reproductive body, the body that thwarts life, the queer death drive.

embodying the queer ghost means that one acknowledges one's position while acknowledging that one is *placed* into that position – i am certainly going to die and fuck you!

in embodying a queer ghost i attempt thwart the modes of life that place me here.
        (situated or placed across something else)

can one use proximity to death as a weapon? as a mode of transportation? as a way of disrupting the life that places one close to death?

at risk of didacticism i begin to answer questions:

*can one bridge, abut, or be situated across life and death?*

how can one not? the only unique aspect of life is that it always-already contains and returns to non-life. that is, all life eventually ends, but not all life eventually starts. that is, what is alive must die, but what is not-alive needn't necessarily become alive.

*why not?*

life seeks to re-embody itself, in some senses. not to suggest that we as living things <u>must</u> reproduce, but that we may. reflection is necessary here. scientific thought, which is too often uncritically reproduced, has centered the study of life on dna – the ultimate repro-ductive machine, autoteleologically copying itself-for-itself.

the reproductive urge seeks subsume all non-life with life. that which is non-life is non-relevant to sheer reproductivity. the smallest unit of meaning is the unit which reproduces itself.

*why embody ghostliness?*

i am certainly going to die, and fuck you

it does no good to deny that the queer is pushed to the margins of society. the queer as a non-reproductive figure seems antithetical to the well-being or continued existence of a society (we are).

the exertion of biopower has put us here. we are in death's backyard. get off my lawn!

*I enjoy life enormously*
*But, of course*
*With my beloved death*
-César Vallejo

it does me no good to deny the proximity of
death. does it do me any good to celebrate my
proximity to death?

i am trying on
death like i try
on your arms
for size

i try death on
in the fitting
rooms eyes
closed rigored
legs –

i am trying on
trying on death
a curse on both
myself and anyone
else in particular
it is snowing
today and i
love you
dearly

*rules number seven through nine of being a ghost—*

must a ghost take a form?
watch your indicative
to take (a form)
to have (a form)
to be (a form)
to give (a form)
to hold (a form)
a foam


must a ghost take/have/be/give/hold a form


what can the ghost give form to?


and here again i am pointing at light
as if i am in a church
and you are in a church too
and we are in a church together
pointing at beams of light

that one is a ghost isn't it?

is it the light or dust in the light

what is the form of the beam

what forms can a ghost take
very many

i am a ghost and i am taking forms

i take the form of the night and i put in my
back pocket

i take the form of the wax drippings and i put
it in my back pocket

i take the form of my back pocket and i put it
in my back pocket

i can fold inside out and outside in, i am very
flexible as a ghost, it means i can collect any
form i think is nice and keep it, this means
i take forms like a magpie takes forms, this
means i get to cackle and scream

what forms can a ghost hold


a ghost cannot hold your form
i have learned this the hard way
i am passing through your form
again and again and again
like water in a glass
i cannot hold shape only
be held by a shape
and you don't stand a
chance of holding this shape


a ghost cannot hold this form
no
it is unfortunate
but you did know that already


a ghost can hold
the form of a
shout across a void or
place
*hey!*

*a body as the house —*


we throw open the goddamn windows
it is too beautiful not to
have you seen the way dead trees
sometimes grow one tiny leaf
i once saw a cactus fall over dead
but bloom each spring
for three years


no one tells you
how death is supposed to fit
no one tells you
that you can get death tailored
at really any dry cleaners


no one tells you
how you can occupy space
in so many ways
i am hanging on
cobwebs in the corners
and hollering
out the open windows

death blows in and out of our house
the shutters shudder
how apt


*but also the haunting—*


we leave
ourselves
for there to be

a trail of salt
leading up the walk


or a space between
or across

our bodies

and our ghosts

proximate


to
death
the never lived

clatter the plates
in the cupboards
a little bit would you

*rule number ten of being a ghost—*

when you throw the windows open
it gets cold

when you throw the body open
it gets cold

when you throw the river open
it gets cold

when a ghost becomes a form
it gets cold

when life becomes non-life
it gets cold

when we point at beams of light in a church
it gets cold

you get the point

*rule number eleven of being a ghost—*

disinhabitation

this is somewhere between
being at home anywhere
and being at home nowhere
but it is definitely not
being at home somewhere

i don't mean to be so opaque
but a ghost sees herself
in a stained glass mirror
remember?

let's try it:

there is a ghost in your house
you are sure of this
you would like to meet the ghost
wouldn't anyone
here
put your fingers together
hold your own heat in your palm
it gets cold
your physical body is now:

*the coldest windowpane in the house*
*the third step*
*the smell of baking bread*
*dust, etc.*
*ache*

the body of yours meets the body of the
ghost
you remember
having had another body
and the way it felt
you take this feeling
out of your ex-mouth
where it sat like a marble
and you put it into the
ex-mouth of the ghost
(presuming this ghost had a mouth)
and you both chew
with mouths you do not have
and have never had

this is the first bridge

to the ghost
the first stained glass window
you have ever seen
one huge sheet
of green light
caught in its own throat
you have a huge sheet
of green light
caught in your throat

and now that you
aren't a ghost anymore
(were you ever)
this sheet of green light
takes the form
(holds the form, is the form)
of both feeling and memory
that says without saying –


there was another place
there is another place
there can be another place
there will be another place
there must be another place

there may be another place

*rule number twelve of being a ghost—*

there may be another place
and this can be
all i mean to suggest
with ghostliness
there may be another place

a place where i
can dip a ladle into
death and see the
ways it hides from me
where i can
have a queer death
practice without
queerness implying
death –

there can be another
place where every house
is haunted and haunting
haunt from *hanter*
to busy oneself with/
to be familiar with/
to indulge in/

the haunting of a house
to indulge in a house
to be familiar with
a body any body this body as body
i busy myself with the haunted house
a house that indulges itself


there may be another place
where a house does and undoes itself
where a body does and undoes itself
where the line
between house    and    body
slips out from itself

the body that is its own escape
the shout
there may be another place
like this

*rule number thirteen of being a ghost—*


thirteen isn't a magic number or anything
yr thinking of the number three



we live together in a big haunted house
all the windows are stained glass
except for the mirror
you can see right out into the
yard through the mirror
and it's always misty and the
trees but
anyway
it's a big house and we
throw the windows open
every morning and laugh
when the rain
in and ruins the carpets
we keep a heavy
wooden table close
and a butter knife
with a weightiness to it

37

we spread fruits on
toast you feed me
figs from your
ghost hand and i
eat figs off of your
ghost body and i
holler out the mirror
into the yard –
we are ghosts
in the house and it
is always sunday
and the mold and
the moss grow
their slow growth
in the books and the
floors but they
are soft and we
let them the books
turn into moss
one by one and
you laugh a clear
laugh like the sun
on a fresh snow
this is called haunting

sometimes the neighborhood
kids come hiking all
the way up the hill and
poke around and we
throw plates and
cackle and hold
candles in our teeth
and laugh and laugh
and the neighborhood kids
laugh too but we
turn them into birds
and they perch in the
dead tree in the front yard
for a while and then
we turn them back
and they know that
it's going to be okay
and they go home
to wherever kids live
these days
              you know
an empty house is never
empty long our haunted
house is full of the
idea of a house and
we are full of the

ideas of ghosts
this is a blessing
we tell each other
what it means to
be blessed
even though we
are trickster ghosts
i tell you about
a blessing in a plastic
bag and convenience store
coffee and so
much quiet such
a big field of quiet they
farm quiet around
here it's the best
quiet anyone ever
saw gotdam
and you tell me about
blessing like a tender
joint and a sound
that fell like a page
like a leaf like a dusk
right into your lap
my lap any lap this
sound of a falling blessing
we stay up late trying to

make the blessing sound
with our own ghost
mouths but it sounds
like wind and we laugh
and that sound like wind too
and we close the windows
so we can
throw them open first thing
in the morning and
laugh this is how
it is to be a ghost

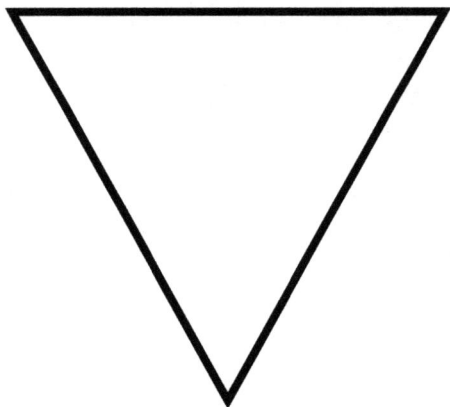

?

*how to stop being a ghost—*

we don't
need to talk about
your reasons


but you should
know


there are only two options –

being a ghost
or being pursued by ghosts


by this i mean to say
yes, i will pursue you

but
more than this


there are so many ways
that life has been foul to us
that we have been hurt
by people and groups of
people and the idea of groups
of people
being a ghost is not
a way of giving up
anything at all
it can be a way of
drawing strength


(i am certainly going to die! and fuck you!)


you may choose to
stop being a ghost
but keep in mind
you cannot chose
to never have been
a ghost

nor can you choose
to escape the ghosts
that will now pursue
your uncorpse the
ways you take up
space will be haunted
by the ways that we
(or i or us) do not
take up space and
the spaces we do
not take up
these things will
be shouted to you
on the other side
in place, situated
where you choose
to stand. where
will you choose to
stand?


i choose to
never have been
not a ghost
i have been haunting
this house

forever
i was haunting this
house before it was built
i was haunting individual trees
and sand for glass
and ore for copper and
steel
and cotton for fiber
knowing that it would be
a house one day
i mean this exact house
and before that i haunted
what would be the trees
and so on

these things come together
and fall apart
ceaselessly
and
again and over

if you stop being a ghost
i will still throw open
these windows and
laugh every morning
and eventually
i will haunt the dust
that this house becomes

my queerness is a stain
on this physical universe!
i will never not haunt you!
this is a literal statement –
i do not want to buy a house
i want to be a house and
the haunting of a house
and i want to throw plates
at every one of your dumb heads
and haunt rocks and
haunt trash until the
universe ends and i will
have haunted it !
there may be another place!

you may choose to stop being a ghost
it is honestly pretty simple

one clear and cold morning
we throw open the windows
you put on your pants
and walk out of the house
and walk out of the corners of the house
and walk out of the mirror
and the books all mossed
and the table we eat fruits at
you walk out of all these things
at the same time
you pick a spot
any it doesn't matter
the house you and the books you and the
table you all walk into the same spot
and the stones you once haunted and the
dust you would have come to haunt
all walk into the same spot
and that's that.

after this you should find a job
or a place to put your body
after this you should find a coat
and good socks
it gets cold after all
my love it gets so cold

## acknowledgments

in the memory of every queer
person who died too soon
and the ones who keep living
despite every cop who hasn't
died soon enough

to kit - for all the houses we've
haunted and are to haunt.

to jane — a joy to point at
ghosts with you.

jasper avery is a poet from arizona pursuing an MFA at Temple University in philadelphia. she has previously published a chapbook, *ghost medicine*, through glowworm press. her debut full length collection, *number one earth*, is the winner of the 2017 Metatron Prize and will be available in 2018.

## Other very fine titles from Trident Press:

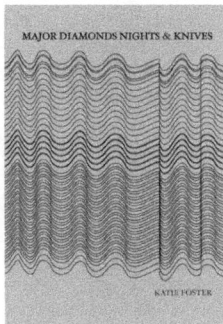

www.ingramcontent.com/pod-product-compliance
Lightning Source LLC
Chambersburg PA
CBHW051039030426
42336CB00015B/2956